Jack & Reg Absalom

OUTBACK
COOKING
IN THE
Camp Oven

Jack & Reg Absalom

OUTBACK COOKING
IN THE
Camp Oven

Photography by
Jocelyn Burt

The Five Mile Press

The Five Mile Press Pty Ltd
22 Summit Road
Noble Park Victoria 3174 Australia

First published in 1982
This paperback edition first published in 1990
Reprinted 1991, 1993, 1994 (twice), 1995, 1996
Text copyright © Pitinjarra Pty Ltd 1982
Photography copyright © Jocelyn Burt 1982
All rights reserved.

Designed by Derrick I. Stone Design
Printed in Singapore by KHL Printing Co.

National Library of Australia
Cataloguing-in-Publication data
Absalom, Jack, 1927- .
Outback cooking in the camp oven
ISBN 0 86788 281 6
I. Outdoor cookery. 2. Cookery, Australian.
I. Absalom, Reg. II. Burt, Jocelyn. III. Title
641.5782

Contents

Introduction   7
Photographers Comment   9
Camp Ovens   11
Funny Stories   17

Soups   23
Starters   25
Quick Meals   27
Fish   33
Meat   40
Curries   58
Poultry & Game   60
Cooking in foil   67
Vegetables as side dishes   72
Sauces & Gravies   75
Desserts   80
Pastries   87
Cakes & Biscuits   92
Dumplings, Scones & Bread   96
Batters   102
Yeasts   104
Pickles, Chutneys & Brines   108

Reg Absalom preparing buns.

Introduction

During my first television series in which I did four cooking scenes, I received many letters asking for recipes on how to cook kangaroo, wild goat and wild pigs. After thinking about this, I decided to write this book and show people how to use camp ovens for cooking in the outback.

I have an uncle, Reg Absalom, who has spent his whole life cooking on stations, in shearing sheds and on bush camps. He is without peer as a cook. Everything is cooked beautifully in the camp oven. Many times in the bush when I have introduced myself to people, they have said, "Absalom, would you be related to Reg Absalom?" When I have said, "Yes he is my uncle", always their next statement is "Can that bloke cook!" Then they relate some story of his talents.

So when I decided to write this book I contacted Reg and suggested we do it together.

All the contents are bush recipes, in most cases with wonderful bush names. I have not set out to write a fancy cook book, but one that is truly Australian, using the foods that are available in most tucker boxes in the outback of Australia. I am sure that you will find it very helpful for travelling the bush. Also you will have a lot of fun trying out the recipes in the camp oven.

Reg and I have tried to give you different ways to cook a lot of the foods that are available in the outback, such as rabbit, kangaroo, wild ducks, wild peaches (quondongs) and fish such as perch and yella belly, not forgetting yabbies. For real flavour in food a camp oven stands supreme. Anybody that has tasted wild ducks cooked in a camp oven will always remember it. We show you how to make pastries for several different dishes, yeasts and cakes and top quality bread. How to use the yeast available in stores and how to make your own yeast. How to make your own brine to corn your meat. How to make colourings to colour gravies and sauces. And very importantly how to tell the temperature in the camp oven. After you have been cooking in a camp oven for a week or so you will find no problems at all. We show you the different types of camp ovens, and why some people prefer one to the other.

Many times when I have spoken to people who are going to make their first camping trip, they have expressed the fact that they don't know how they are going to handle cooking on an open fire. Well I promise you that after you have read this book, all your fears of bush cooking will disappear and be replaced with pleasure and satisfaction with the results that you get.

Most of the recipes that Reg has supplied for the book have comments at the end of them, such as "very tasty" or "very nice". I have left these as he gave them to me because I think this is part of the outback way of saying things. While we were doing the photography for the book with Jocelyn Burt, we cooked every recipe in the camp oven or in the coals. Then we ate them for our meals. It has been one of the most enjoyable tasks I have ever undertaken and if I have a complaint it is that I have put on too much weight.

Good cooking,
Jack Absalom

Photographer's Comment

When I was first asked to do the photography for this book, I rather wondered what I was in for with Jack and Reg Absalom. For one wild moment I thought that I might be expected to eat cooked witchetty grubs, snakes, sugar ants and other bush "delicacies". To my delight (and relief) I discovered that the recipes contained nothing but good, wholesome ingredients — including the meat from kangaroos and feral animals, which were excellent eating. If certain species of kangaroo must be shot in order to prevent plague proportions developing on farms and stations, why should our pets be the only ones to enjoy this delectable meat?

Before meeting the Absaloms, I knew very little about the camp oven, so I had much to learn. What astonished me the most was its versatility. This bush stove cooks all the same type of dishes that the domestic stove cooks — including the lightest sponge! I was also very impressed with the economy of this practical utensil. Like many outback travellers, I generally stick to expensive gas cooking on my field trips, using a fire only for barbecuing meat and for sitting around. Think of the coals wasted!

Previously, my only taste of true outback recipes had been damper, mostly made in the coals by clueless safari drivers who were expected to produce it immediately after the evening meal in a floor show-like activity for the entertainment of the passengers. A damper that one enthusiastic person attempted to make bore a remarkable resemblance to a black cricket ball. Damper is one food that all prospective outback travellers should be prepared to make, because if breakdowns or other delays occur and the bread supply is exhausted, it is the perfect substitute. I have never had such good damper as Reg Absalom's; indeed, his damper scones were a positive threat to my waistline.

This assignment was full of joy and fun for me, and I could not have had better tutors in the art of camp oven cooking. Reg would surely be one of the most experienced bush cooks in Australia, and Jack's enthusiasm was so infectious that after finishing the photography, I immediately placed an order for a camp oven at the nearest hardware store. After reading their book, I think you will too!

JOCELYN BURT

9

The above photo shows our camp ovens that we used to cook the recipes in this book. The two front ones are Bedourie ovens. These are made of pressed steel, generally favoured on stations today because they are unbreakable. The five ovens at the back are the common cast iron camp ovens that have been the most used cooking utensil in the outback of Australia since the first settlement. Because they are made of cast iron, they have to be looked after properly, and always packed safely for travelling. I have had my three cast iron ovens for over 30 years.

The photo below shows all the camp ovens being used at one time. The boiler that is first on the left contained boiling water. Reg was inspecting the Roast Spare Ribs.

10

Camp Ovens

Most people think that the camp ovens which we have today were only made in the last hundred years or so, when in actual fact they were in use before we had the fuel burning stoves such as wood stoves and coal stoves. People in underdeveloped countries today still do their cooking on open fires using boilers and cast iron ovens with lids. These camp ovens come in different shapes and sizes.

The Bedourie camp oven made of pressed steel with the lid that fits over the top was made for Bedourie Station. This station found that when the cast iron camp ovens fell off the packed horses, or were dropped, they often broke, so they invented the Bedourie, which would not break.

The above photo shows a typical bush scene. Coals have been taken from the main fire and camp ovens placed on them. Then a windbreak of branches have been placed next to the camp oven to stop the breeze fanning the coals and causing a hot spot under the oven. If the wind is causing problems, use branches or a piece of tin if available. Also turn your camp oven around to a different position so the hot spot is moved to the other side. After a little experience with these types of problems you will handle them with ease.

11

It served the same purposes for cooking except for bread, cakes or similar foods. To keep the heat in you had to half bury the Bedourie in hot ashes with some coals then add further coals to the lid and it would cook just as well as the cast iron camp ovens. The Bedourie has one very good point in that the lid fits down over the oven, so when you bury the camp oven there is no chance of the ashes getting into the oven. Also the lid may be turned over and used as a frying pan.

The main thing you have to watch when cooking with a camp oven is that it doesn't need many coals underneath, or on the lid, to cook most dishes. I always put the oven on the main fire to heat it up first, then when placed on the coals it has plenty of heat. Again, when you are cooking and you need heat from above for such foods as bread, pastries and cakes, get the lid very hot on the fire then when you put it on the camp oven, you have heat immediately. This way you will only need a few coals to retain the heat.

Never pour cold water in a hot camp oven because it will crack. When you want to wash your camp oven out always use hot or warm water. After you have washed the oven put a little oil or fat inside and wipe it around. By doing this your oven will never rust, and if you have kept the lid on, it will always be clean and only need wiping out with a damp cloth before cooking.

It is advisable to have a couple of wire hooks, about 24" long, for lifting the lid off the oven and for moving the camp oven around.

When travelling with your camp oven I suggest you have a cardboard box roughly the same size as your camp oven to keep it in. Place a piece of foam rubber or cloth between the lid and the oven. By doing this you avoid the chance of a bad jolt causing the lid to fly up and come down breaking your camp oven. And also if you carry it in a carton you will not get black all over everything it touches.

When cooking and there is a breeze blowing, place something on the ground, like a piece of tin to stop the wind hitting the camp oven. If you let the breeze fan the coals you could get a hot spot, which will burn your food at this point. See photograph on next page. Also if you find your oven getting too hot in one spot move it around.

You will find within a couple of days of camp oven cooking you will handle it like a veteran. If it starts raining place something over the top of your oven like a piece of tin or even the blade of your shovel. This is to stop the rain from hitting the oven and cooling it down. I have cooked in a camp oven with it pouring rain and all these things can be handled with a little thought.

Always make a good fire so there is plenty of coals available to do your cooking with. I love Mulga wood, it always gives a good fire with good coals that last. Some wood such as Pine, flares up and burns then goes to ash leaving very little coals.

OVEN HEATS BY PAPER TEST

Place a piece of paper inside the oven to find out what heat the oven is at.

Heat	Degrees	Paper Test
very hot oven	500	dark brown
hot oven	375-400	light brown
moderate oven	325-375	yellow
slow oven	250-325	crust

Too bloody hot — black and on fire

The photo above shows Reg adding a few more coals to the lid of the camp oven; it's so easy. If you want a little more heat from the top just add a few more coals. If it is cooking too fast just take some off.

The photo above shows Reg using the camp oven irons to lift the camp oven off the coals. The irons are part of your camp oven cooking, always keep them with your oven.

14

The photo above shows Reg lifting the lid off the camp oven to inspect the pumpkin
scones. A little practise will make you competent at doing this.

Funny Stories

This was many years ago when there were big shearing sheds. In Dunlop in N.S.W. there was about 100 shearers, 12 cooks and 150 station hands and rousabouts. And there was over 100,000 sheep. Then there was the usual new chum rolling up at shearing time looking for a job like everybody else. So he asked the manager if there was any work at the station. "Sorry" said the boss "but we are full up! But", he said, "there might be a job over at the cooks' quarters." Away he went to see the cooks about a job.

Arriving at the kitchen they could see that he was a new chum so they said "have a pint of tea mate", "thanks" said the new chum. The cooks got together, they thought they would have a joke with the new chum, so they asked him if he wanted a job. "Sure" said the new chum. "Well the only job we have is to stir the porridge at breakfast time; you start about 3.30". "O.K." said the new chum, "show me the pot with the porridge in so I know it in the morning." "You can't mistake it", said one cook, "there is only one boat you have to row out and keep stirring till breakfast time."

CLEANING SAUSAGES

A chap wanted to be a shearers' cook so I said "O.K., cook on a station for a while and then come and see me."

Ten months later he came and said "I reckon I can make it now, so put some meat on the table and I'll see if I can cook it and pass the test." So next morning I dropped a parcel of meat on the table and he said "what's that?" and I said "sausages" and he said "how do you cook them?" I replied "like fish", so he took them outside and cleaned them.

THE NEW COOK

Years ago on Naryilco Station they were getting a camp ready to go out for a month and muster the western part of the run. They had a new cook who had only arrived the day before, nobody knew of his ability, anyway away they went.

After two days all the boys in the camp were complaining about the terrible meals they were getting, so they approached the boss who was the manager, a Harold Hickson. They said that they could not take the cooking, Harold

17

said "O.K. I will sack the cook, but who is going to do the cooking?" and he looked at the men. He said "Come on, speak up! Who is going to do the cooking?" Nobody wanted the job so he said "All right! I will go cook, but I warn you somebody will want to cook tomorrow."

That evening he mixed some flour and water till it was heavy dough, then pulled pieces off the size of a tennis ball and threw them on the coals. He then took a big lump of meat and proceeded to cut off pieces the same size as the dough and toss them all over the coals in the fire. He then called out "come and get it", and that was dinner. Needless to say one of the boys was the cook next day. Harold said "I told you I was a terrible cook."

JACK ABSALOM

THE SHEARERS' COOK

The shearing had started, everybody was happy, they had a marvellous cook. This night he had cooked a roast, with roast potatoes, beans, peas and onions. As is the custom in most sheds the men file along the table and take what they want off each dish. This particular shearer came to the end of the table and said "where is the gravy?" There was none, the cook had forgotten to make it. The shearer walked to the dining room moaning, "bloody cooks that half do their jobs." Then while he is sitting down eating the meal he kept saying "darn good meal spoilt because of no gravy." After about 15 minutes of this the cook grabbed a piece of pine flooring board about 6 feet long that was in the kitchen. He walked into the dining room over to the complaining shearer, crashed the board down on his head and said "try that for gravy." Then he looked all around the table at the other men and said "does anybody else want some gravy while I am here!!"

JACK ABSALOM

RHUBARB PIE

This chap wrote to me and asked if I would recommend him for a cook's job in the team. He said he was a cook, so while I was in town I met up with him. He seemed O.K. from what I could gather as a cook. I promised him I would do what I could. When the opportunity came I got him the job on the station I was working on.
We got breakfast over with, we had chops and eggs which seemed all right on his first day. And he arranged a cold lunch. He asked me after lunch "what do they have for the evening meal?" So I outlined a few dishes and one was

18

rhubarb pie, because I had seen a lot of rhubarb in the cool room. I said "make a rhubarb pie with custard, you'll see it in the cool room." I told him it was the long red stuff. "O.K." he replied.

So came the evening meal. As I like rhubarb I was ready for my share, I said "David, where's the rhubarb pie?" Bugger the pie" he said, "I wasted all the afternoon looking for a dish long enough to put it in!"

REG ABSALOM

ROASTED APPLES

Then there was another chap left in the camp to do the cooking for the day. I gave him instructions on what there was to cook. I said "roast a leg of mutton, with roast potatoes and cook some cabbage. For sweets you may as well cook some apples (as we had plenty) and make a custard."

So home we came ready and hungry. I started cutting off some meat and getting the potatoes and onions out of the camp oven.

I said "What the hell is this?"

He replied "You said to bake the apples also."

He had roasted them!

REG ABSALOM

Two Typically Australian Dishes

Recommended by this office for serving to V.I.P. visitors

BARBECUED EMU

Take 1 young hen — stretch neck.
Remove some feathers for decoration.

Have prepared a goodly-sized hole of white ash and coals.
Place bird on same, and cover with green boughs.
Cook until feathers gone and skin golden brown.
Rub with mallee (green) roots to remove quills.

Serve to old men and dogs, then the women and kids.
                    DELICIOUS!

CAMEL STEW

3 medium sized camels
1 ton salt
1 ton pepper
500 bushels potatoes
200 bushels carrots
3000 sprigs parsley
2 small rabbits

Cut camels into bite size pieces. This should take about two months.
Cut vegetables into cubes (another two months).
Place meat in pan and cover with 1000 gallons of brown gravy.
Simmer for 4 weeks.
Shovel in pepper and salt to taste.
When meat is tender, add vegetables.
Simmer slowly for 4 weeks.
Garnish with parsley.
Will serve 3800 people.
If more are expected, add two rabbits.

These two recipes were given to me by a manager of one of Kidmans Stations. He told me that the Head Office in Adelaide sent these two recipes to all his stations.
P.S. I haven't tried them, as I have had trouble getting the three medium sized camels.

Jack Absalom

Kangaroo Tail Soup.

22

Soups

1 kangaroo tail
2 onions
1 tin tomato soup
1½ cups spaghetti
salt and pepper to taste

SPAGHETTI SOUP

Cooking time: 20 minutes.

Boil kangaroo tail or joints until tender, with chopped onions. When cooked add tomato soup and spaghetti, simmer until tender, about 20 minutes. Add salt and pepper.

1 kg/2 lbs fish
1 cup vinegar
½ cup olive oil
4 cups water
1 potato chopped
1 onion chopped
parsley
cornflour to thicken
salt and pepper to taste

YELLA BELLY SOUP (fish)

Cooking time: 40-60 minutes

Clean fish. Place in dish and add vinegar, olive oil or other oil and the water. Boil until cooked. When ready drain off liquid and add potato, onion and parsley. Now thicken with the cornflour. Add salt and pepper.

6 joints of kangaroo tail
any vegetables you may have
noodles, macaroni or spaghetti
1 cup split peas
2 onions
salt and pepper to taste

KANGAROO TAIL SOUP

Cooking time: 3 hours.

Place the tail in an 8 pint saucepan or camp oven. Cover with water and bring to the boil. When boiling, place in split peas, onions and noodles, macaroni or spaghetti. Boil until all is cooked along with the meat. Add the vegetables you have diced up, whether they be fresh, tinned or dried. Cook until these are tender then add your salt and pepper.

This is one of my favourite dishes in the bush and I never get sick of it.

Jack Absalom.

LIGHTNING RIDGE GALAH SOUP

3 galahs
any diced vegetables
potato (optional)
onion (optional)
cornflour
salt and pepper to taste

Cooking time: 2 hours

The galahs must be skinned. Cut along the breast, pull the skin off with the feathers on. Then cut off the legs, wings and the breast of the galah. Place these in camp oven and cover with water, boil until tender, about 1½ hours. Now place the vegetables in and boil until the soup is creamy. If not thick enough add a little cornflour, then the salt and pepper.

WILD DUCK SOUP

1 duck
2 onions
1 tin tomato soup
1 capsicum, red or green
½ cup rice
salt and pepper to taste

Cooking time: 3 hours.

Cut duck up into pieces and boil with the onions diced. When well cooked add tomato soup, capsicum and rice. Boil until well cooked then add salt and pepper.

Starters

yabbies (as many as required)
fat or oil for frying
2 beaten eggs
1½ cups breadcrumbs

BROKEN HILL'S FAMOUS CRUMBED YABBIES

Cooking time: 10 minutes.

Cook and clean yabbies, take the tails only. Roll tails in flour then in the eggs. Pick them out with tongs or fingers and roll in breadcrumbs. Drop in boiling fat or oil and cook until they are brown. Lift out. Very tasty.

1 dozen yabbies per person
lettuce

YABBIE COCKTAILS

Sauce
½ cup cream
1 tbls hot sauce
2 tbls tomato sauce
1 teas lemon juice
salt and pepper to taste

The yabbies must be cooked, use the tails only. Get as many small bowls as required. Place a leaf of lettuce in the base of each and fill with yabbie tails. Pour a generous amount of sauce on each one. Ready to serve.

2 dozen large yabbie tails
6 slices bacon

YABBIE KEBABS

Cooking time: 10 minutes.

Cut bacon in strips, half length wise. Wrap each yabbie tail in bacon, put on a skewer and grill over hot coals.

I always find that when I take children into the bush, I get a lot of enjoyment out of watching them make their own kebabs. I am sure they also get a lot of fun making their rack to cook them on out of twigs and doing the cooking themselves.

Jack Absalom.

25

Yabbie Kebabs.

Quick Meals

500 g/1 lb elbow macaroni
2 tbls butter
salt and pepper
chopped parsley

SCRAMBLED EGGS BUSH STYLE

Cooking time: 30 minutes.

Boil the macaroni until it is nearly cooked then let it stand in the hot water for 1 hour with the lid on. Drain off the water thoroughly. Place the butter in the camp oven, when it has melted add the macaroni and fry. Keep stirring. Add the salt and pepper to taste and some chopped parsley. Serve on buttered toast.

oil for frying
6 slices thick bread
1 teas salt
¼ teas pepper
6 eggs

HOLE IN ONE EGG

Cooking time: 15 minutes.

Put oil in camp oven and heat. Cut centres from the bread using a scone cutter or doughnut cutter, keep for croutons. Place prepared bread in oven. Break an egg and drop it in the hole of the bread. Also fry the centres of bread. Keep turning the bread until it is a nice brown then lift out and do the rest the same way. Add a little more oil if needed.

3 eggs
salt and pepper to taste
nob of butter

ROO SHOOTERS' OMELET

Cooking time: 10 minutes.

Break the eggs into a bowl and beat with a fork until well broken up. Heat camp oven, use a small oven if you have one. Smear the base of the oven with the butter then stir in the eggs. When in the oven stir about lightly with a fork. When set fold the omelet in half and leave a little longer until well heated, remove from oven and serve at once.

27

BIRDSVILLE SPAGHETTI

½ pkt spaghetti
2 large onions
2 large tomatoes
1 tbls margarine
½ cup tomato sauce
1 teas salt
1½ teas pepper
stock or water (optional)
1 cup grated cheese

Cooking time: 30-40 minutes.

Boil the spaghetti for 10 minutes, remove from the heat and let stand for 20 minutes to seep (soften up). Dice the onions and tomatoes. Fry the onions in the margarine until brown, now add the tomatoes and tomato sauce, salt and pepper. Strain off spaghetti and mix together. Add a little stock or water if too dry. Serve with grated cheese.

NULLABOR PLAINS MOCK FISH

oil for frying
3 potatoes
3 eggs well beaten
1 dessertspoon flour
salt and pepper to taste

Cooking time: 10-15 minutes.

Peel the potatoes and grate into a bowl. In another bowl mix the beaten eggs, flour, salt and pepper. Now squeeze out any water from the potatoes and add this to the egg mixture. Have oil hot in oven, not too much, as much as you would use to cook an egg. Spoon mixture in and fry until brown. Serve for breakfast.

This recipe is a great stand-by in the bush. I remember my mother making these on many occasions. I always love them pressed thin and browned up nice and crisp, with tomato sauce.

Jack Absalom.

A QUICK HOT MEAL

cold cooked meat (any type)

Gravy
1 cup water
1 dessertspoon cornflour
1½ tbls hot sauce

1 tbls port (optional)
salt and pepper to taste

Cooking time: 10-15 minutes.

Mix all ingredients for gravy together and heat in the camp oven. When hot, drop in as much meat as you wish. Cook until gravy is a nice thickness. Serve with desired vegetables.

500 g/1 lb minced meat
1 teas mixed herbs
1 clove garlic
salt and pepper
1 egg

PARTY MEAT ROLL

Short Crust Pastry
250 g/½ lb flour
125 g/¼lb butter
½ cup water
pinch of salt

Cooking time: 30 minutes.

To make the pastry sift the flour, add salt and rub butter in lightly with finger tips. Pour the water in the centre slowly making a stiff dough that will leave the sides of the dish clearly. Tip out on a floured board and knead with finger tips and thumbs. Turn rough side down and roll out to 12" by 6" roughly Mix together minced meat, mixed herbs, garlic, salt and pepper. Place meat on pastry and roll up. Put on a meat tray or in the camp oven and paint with beaten egg. Bake in hot oven for 30 minutes until brown.

cold cooked meat
any vegetables you have
oil

BRUMBIES IN THE SANDHïLLS

Batter
2 cups S.R. flour
pinch of salt
milk
1 egg

Cooking time: 10 minutes.

Place flour, salt and the egg in a bowl. Mix well slowly adding a little milk at a time until you have a smooth batter. Mince all your meat and veggies up together and mix into the batter. Have oil hot in camp oven. Spoon mixture into the hot oil. Turn them when edges look like crumpets that are bubbly. Fry till golden brown. Serve as they are or with bacon and eggs.

This is another very quick meal using all your left over meat and veg. Easy to make and a good meal.

Brumbies in the Sandhills.

Jack Absalom.

slices of cold cooked meat
oil for frying

Batter
2 cups S.R. flour
pinch salt
1 egg
milk

Cooking time: 10 minutes.

Place flour, egg and salt in a bowl. Mix well slowly adding
a little milk until you have a smooth batter. Have the oil
hot in the camp oven. Dip half inch slices of cold meat into
the batter and then drop them into the hot oil. When cooked
and brown take out and place on a piece of paper. Now
ready to serve.
If you do not have fresh cold meat a tin of camp pie will
substitute.

*This is a wonderful, quick meal in the bush. Any cold meat may
be used or even a tin of luncheon meat or bully beef. They always
taste good.*

Jack Absalom.

OPAL BUYERS'
OMELET

3 eggs
1 dessertspoon flour
salt and pepper to taste
2 strips of bacon chopped finely
4 green onions (chives or shallots) chopped finely
3 sprigs parsley or dried flakes
nob of butter

Cooking time: 10 minutes.

Get oven hot. Beat the eggs, add the flour and all other ingredients except the butter. When mixed well place the butter in the bottom of the camp oven. Pour in the omelet mixture and bake until set and slightly brown.
Also, if you have some mushrooms or tomatoes you can use these as a filling. Place on the omelet before folding over. Warm tomatoes or mushrooms or any solid filling either on griller or in oven with a little butter.

Fish

3 yella belly

FENCERS' CURRIED FISH

Sauce
1 large onion, chopped
1 large capsicum, sliced
1 stick celery, chopped
1 small tin pineapple pieces
1 large carrot, chopped
2 tbls margarine
1 tbls curry powder
1 can tomato soup
salt and pepper to taste

Cooking time: 2 hours.

Clean fish and partly cook in water. Take out and place in the camp oven or dish that will fit in camp oven. Place margarine in camp oven. When this is melted add the capsicum, celery, carrot and the onion. Cook for 20 minutes, keep stirring. When nearly cooked add the pineapple strained, keep the juice for later. Now stir in the curry powder, salt and pepper. Mix together for another 10 minutes then add the rest of the ingredients, tomato soup and the pineapple juice. Do not make too thin. When all mixed pour over the fish and place in camp oven on low heat for 1 hour. Serve with rice and chopped boiled eggs.

1 1 kg/2 lbs yella belly per person

CRUMBED FISH DROVERS' STYLE

Batter
2 eggs
pinch of salt
1 large tbl flour
milk

Cooking time: 15-20 minutes.

Clean and fillet the fish. Cut into pieces. Now make the batter. Beat the eggs with the salt. Mix the flour with a little milk and add it to the eggs. Keep beating until you have a nice batter that will pour from a jug. If too thick add a little more milk or if too thin a little more flour. For best

33

results let the batter stand for 1 hour before using. When ready dip the pieces of fish into the batter and have hot about 1½ inches of oil or fat in the bottom of the camp oven. Drop the fish in until cooked. Do not over cook, allow about 10 minutes until nice and golden brown.

OPAL MINERS' FISH IN WHITE SAUCE

1 medium-large size fish

White Sauce

2 cups milk
1 tbls plain flour
salt and pepper to taste
1 teas chopped or dried parsley
1 nob butter

Garnish
chopped or dried parsley
lemon slices
parmesan cheese

Cooking time: 10-15 minutes.

Scale and clean fish, fillet if required, if not place in strainer or on perforated dish as this will keep the fish from breaking when nearly cooked. Now that you have the fish in the strainer place this in a large pot with about 1½ inches of water. When the water comes to the boil, boil for a few minutes then take out. Now make the white sauce. Place the milk in a saucepan and bring it to the boil, have ready the flour mixed with a little milk, just enough to make it a liquid. Stir this into the boiling milk until the mixture becomes thick. Add the salt and pepper and put in the parsley with the nob of butter to stop the parsley forming on top. Pour the sauce over the fish and garnish with the parsley, parmesan cheese and lemon slices. If preferred when this is ready place it back in the camp oven, put the lid on with coals on top and brown the cheese. This is delicious.

FISH MORNAY

2 cups cooked fish with bones removed
1 cup rice
1 tbls lemon juice
2 tbls chopped parsley
1 cup soft breadcrumbs   2 tbls butter

34

Opal Miners' Fish in White Sauce.

White Sauce

1 tbl butter
2 tbls cornflour
1½ cups milk
salt and pepper to taste

Cooking time: 30-40 minutes.

Make the white sauce. Melt butter in camp oven or saucepan and mix in cornflour, salt and pepper. Stirring all the time, add the milk until sauce is nice and thick. Now add parsley and lemon juice to white sauce. Place a ½ inch spread of sauce in the bottom of the camp oven or baking dish. Now a layer of fish and then another spread of sauce with the rice on top. Melt the butter and combine with the breadcrumbs. Sprinkle this mixture over the top of the preparation and bake in a hot camp oven for about ½ hour. Serve garnished with parsley.

MIKE McKAY'S CURRIED YABBIES AND RICE

2 dozen big yabbie tails
250 g/½ lb margarine
2 sticks celery, chopped
1 large onion, diced
1 red or green capsicum, sliced
1 small tin pineapple
1 carrot, chopped
1 tbls curry powder
1 tin tomato soup
1 dessertspoon soya sauce
rice (as much as required)
salt and pepper to taste

Cooking time: 2 hours.

Place margarine in camp oven on a slow fire. Put the celery, onion, capsicum and carrot in the camp oven with the pineapple for ½ hour. Now add the curry powder and keep stirring so it will not stick or burn. Cook for about 10 minutes then add the tomato soup to make a good bubbling mixture. Add salt and pepper and soya sauce. If too thick add some pineapple juice. Place in yabbie tails and let simmer over a slow heat for 1 hour. Serve with the boiling rice.

36

2 doz yabbies

Mornay Sauce
1 pint water
2 heaped tbls Sunshine powdered milk
1 tbls cornflower
2 eggs
salt and pepper to taste
½ cup grated cheese
¼ cup breadcrumbs

Cooking time: ½-1 hour.

Cook and clean yabbies, take off the tails and shell. Place
them in a pie dish or in camp oven. Now make the mornay
sauce. Put powdered milk and cornflour in a container and
mix with a little cold water until you have a thickish mixture
that will pour. Place saucepan on coals with the pint of water
and bring to the boil. Remove from heat and add milk
mixture stirring until nice and creamy. Now add the beaten
egg, salt and pepper and stir well. Pour this in pie dish
or camp oven over yabbies and top with cheese and breadcrumbs, heat through. Ready for serving.

*Yabbies make a wonderful change in the bush. And as shown in
the photograph they may be served on a bed of gumleaves.*
                                                    Jack Absalom.

COOPERS STYLE BAKED FISH WHOLE

1 2.25 kg/5 lb fish

Seasoning
2 slices bacon chopped finely
1 onion chopped
1 cup breadcrumbs
1 tomato chopped finely
parsley chopped
1 teas mixed spices
salt and pepper to taste

Garnish
4 slices lemon
1 onion sliced in rings
1 sliced tomato
2 strips bacon

Cooking time: 45 minutes.

Mix all seasoning ingredients together and stuff into fish. Sew or skewer up. Place a sheet of foil in the bottom of the camp oven and place fish on. For the garnish lay the 2 strips of bacon on top of the fish. Throw over the onion rings, slices of tomato and lemon. Bake this in a hot oven until nearly cooked, then fold over the foil so as to steam the fish for the last 10 minutes.

This is a favourite way of cooking whole fish in the bush. Wrap the lot up in foil, then either cook it in the camp oven or bury it.

Jack Absalom.

Meat

MOCK GOOSE KANGAROO LEG ROAST

1 kangaroo leg

Stuffing
1 tin green peas
2 strips bacon
1 onion
1 sheeps kidney
1 teas mint parsley
1 dessertspoon butter

Bread Sauce
1 slice bread per person
1 tbls butter
1 cup milk
salt and pepper

Cooking time: 2½-3 hours.

Bone kangaroo leg. Mix all ingredients of stuffing together, stuff into pocket of kangaroo leg and skewer or sew up. Cook until tender, about 2½-3 hours. Keep the oven hot and sizzling all the time. To make the bread sauce cut crust from bread. Melt the butter in camp oven and add bread cut into small squares. Now add milk, salt and pepper and let boil until thick. Serve kangaroo leg with bread sauce.

MULYUNGARIE KANGAROO AND KIDNEY PIE

2 kangaroo tails
4 large kidneys
2 large onions
4 medium potatoes
2 dessertspoons flour
salt and pepper to taste

Pastry
250 g/½ lb flour
pinch of salt
125 g/4 oz butter
¼-½ cup water

Cooking time: 2 hours.

Joint and wash tail. Place in camp oven, cover with water

40

and cook or simmer for 1½ hours. Cut or dice the kidneys, potatoes and onions. Now place these in camp oven and cook until they are brown. Place the kangaroo tail, kidney and vegetables into a large pie dish which is quite deep. Mix a little flour with the juice from the tail and vegetables, make a nice thick gravy and pour over the lot. Now make the pastry. Sift the flour and salt into a bowl. Chop up all the butter and rub it through the flour. Keep crumbling the flour and butter together while adding a little water at a time, until you have a nice dough. Roll out onto floured board and place on top of kidney pie. Bake in a moderate oven with coals on the lid for about 20-30 minutes.

Mulyungarie Kangaroo and Kidney Pie.

ABSALOM STYLE — KANGAROO LEG SEASONED

1 kangaroo leg
1 cup dripping

Stuffing
½ loaf bread
1 large onion, chopped finely
2 strips bacon, chopped finely
2 soft tomatoes, chopped finely
1 dessertspoon mixed herbs
1 egg
salt and pepper to taste

Cooking time: 2½-3 hours.

Take the kangaroo leg and cut pockets well into the leg so as to push the stuffing in. To make the stuffing cut the crust off the bread and crumb it. Add the bacon, onion and tomatoes. Rub well together with the breadcrumbs then add the egg, mix well, adding herbs then salt and pepper and stuff this into pocket of kangaroo leg. Bake in camp oven with the cup of dripping until well cooked — about 2½-3 hours. Remember to baste the meat all the time because it has no fat.

I have served this meal to governors, millionaires, T.V. crews and hundreds of ordinary people, and I never get a complaint.
Jack Absalom.

OUTBACK BRAISED KANGROO TAIL

1 medium kangaroo tail jointed
2 large onions chopped
2 tbls flour or gravox
salt and pepper to taste
2 carrots, sliced longwise
1 can peas or pkt Surprise peas
3 medium tomatoes, sliced

Cooking time: 1½ hours.

If you have a pressure cooker put the meat in and cook until the meat starts to fall off the bone. Take out and strain off the gravy. Keep it. Place a little fat or butter in the bottom of a hot camp oven and fry the onions until nearly cooked. Strain off some of the fat but leave enough to make a nice gravy. Add either the flour or gravox to the onions to make a nice thick gravy, add the salt and pepper. Place the kangaroo tail in with the onion gravy and add the car-

Roast Leg of Kangaroo.

43

rots, peas and the tomatoes. Tip the onion gravy all over the lot then place lid on camp oven and let simmer for 1½ hours. Serve with mashed potatoes and pieces of pumpkin.

PACKSADDLE KANGAROO BRAWN

2 medium kangaroo tails
water
1 dessertspoon nutmeg
1 dessertspoon mixed spices
salt and pepper to taste

Cooking time: 2-2½ hours.

Clean and joint tails, put them in a pot and cover them with water. Boil until meat is falling off the bone, then pick out the bones with tongs. Now add the nutmeg, mixed herbs, salt and pepper, stir well, breaking up all meat. This should be fairly thick, as long as it has a gravy to taste. Place mixture in pie dish or tray and let set. When ready cut into slices and use for cold lunches or let set in small moulds.

HOT POT

1 kg/2 lb meat (kangaroo, mutton or beef)
4 potatoes
2 onions
4 tomatoes
1 tbl plain flour
1 teas mustard
1 teas plain jam
½ cup tomato paste
1 teas salt
½ teas pepper

Batter
2 cups S.R. flour
1 egg
pinch of salt
milk

Cooking time: approx. 2 hours and 20 minutes.

Place layer of meat in oven. Slice potatoes, onions and tomatoes onto meat, then repeat the process until you have enough. Now mix together the flour, mustard, jam, tomato paste and salt and pepper, with a little water to make a paste. Make enough to come to the top of the prepared. Spoon onto meat and vegetables in camp oven. Let simmer for 2 hours until the meat is tender. Make a batter mixing the flour, beaten egg and salt together with a little milk at a time until you have a nice smooth thickish paste. Pour batter over top of prepared and cook in hot oven placing plenty of coals onto the camp oven lid. When batter is golden brown, after about 15-20 minutes, it is ready to serve.

TRAPPERS' BRAWN WITH KANGAROO TAIL AND SHIN OF BEEF

1 kangaroo tail, jointed
1 shin of beef (medium size)
salt and pepper to taste
2 teas nutmeg
1 teas mixed spices

Cooking time: 1-1½ hours

Place the kangaroo tail and the shin in the oven and cover with water. Cook until meat is falling off the bones. Remove bones. If you have too much liquid take some out, do not throw away, but keep for stock or you may use a little more in the brawn. Add the pepper and salt, nutmeg and mixed spices, stir well, make to taste. Now tray in pie dishes or meat dishes until cool. Leave in dishes until it is all used. It will keep better. Just slice it off as you want it.

LAKE FROME KANGAROO BRAISE

loin of young kangaroo (as much as required)
½ cup plain flour
dripping
4 onions
2 carrots
½ cup peas (dried or canned)
4 tomatoes
flour or gravox
salt and pepper to taste
1 tbls soya sauce

Cooking time: 2½ hours.

Wash and dry meat. Dust with flour. Have dripping hot in oven and drop in each piece of meat. Just brown until both sides are done, then place into a dish. Peel onions and slice. Place the onions in the camp oven. While the onions are cooking place carrots, which have been cleaned

45

and diced, with the peas on top of the meat. Cut up the tomatoes and place them on top of the carrots and peas. When onions are ready, if there is too much fat, drain off a little then add flour or gravox to make a thick gravy and add the soya sauce. Make the gravy rich in colour. Do not make the gravy too thin because you will have the juice from the tomatoes. Take gravy out of the oven and place meat, carrots and tomatoes in the camp oven with the onions. Now pour the sauce over the top and simmer for 2 hours.

This is one of the tastiest braises you can cook in the camp oven, and wonderful to serve on toast for breakfast the next morning.
Jack Absalom.

Lake Frome Kangaroo Braise.

RUDI DUKE'S KANGAROO TAIL STEW WITH DUMPLINGS

2 small kangaroo tails
2 sheep's kidneys
½ cup seasoned flour
1 pint stock
1 oz dripping
1 large onion diced
1 carrot diced
½ turnip diced
1 stick celery diced
3 tbls parsley
salt and pepper to taste

Dumplings
3 cups flour
1 dessertspoon baking powder
1 large teas fat
pinch of salt

Cooking time: 3-4 hours.

Joint kangaroo tails. Skin and halve kidneys. Roll tails and kidneys in seasoned flour and brown in the heated dripping in camp oven. When meat is brown take from camp oven and place in saucepan while you brown the onion, carrot, turnip and celery in the camp oven. When ready add the stock, salt and pepper to the meat and heat. Simmer this for 3 hours. When this is done add the browned veges to the meat and place all in the camp oven for 40 minutes. Now thicken liquid with the plain flour. For dumplings, rub the fat into the flour and baking powder with a little lukewarm water to make a nice soft dough. Add salt and pepper and roll out on floured board. Roll into balls then place on top of your stew. Have the lid on and cook for 20 minutes. Reary to serve.

Kangaroo Tail Stew with Dumplings is a favourite in the bush, especially if you are out of bread, because the dumplings are a good substitute.

Jack Absalom.

KANGAROO KEBABS
1 kg/2 lbs meat (kangaroo)
2 capsicums
2 tomatoes
1 large onion
1 dessertspoon curry powder
½ cup oil
2 tbls hot sauce

Cooking time: 15 minutes.

Dice the meat into 1½ inch cubes, boneless. Finely chop the capsicum, tomatoes and onion. Place these in a bowl with the rest of the ingredients and marinate the meat for 2 hours. Then take out meat and place on skewer and cook over hot coals. Also cook capsicum, tomato, onions and hot sauce in camp oven and serve with kebabs.

Kangaroo Kebabs.

MUNDI MUNDI KANGAROO RISSOLES

1 kg/2 lbs kangaroo meat
2 onions
2 potatoes
1 egg
tomato sauce
salt and pepper

Cooking time: approx. 15-20 minutes.

Cut up small, or mince the meat with the onions and potatoes. Add the salt and pepper. Mix altogether then add the egg for binding. Make into balls and place in camp oven. Place a dessertspoon of tomato sauce on each and bake slowly. Or you can fry them in fat or oil for about 15-20 minutes. Good for breakfast, or for dinner with vegetables.

When I cook these for the evening meal I always cook extra to have cold for lunch the next day. Also a good quick meal to have cold when you're travelling.

Jack Absalom.

Ribs from bullock, goat or sheep
salt and pepper to taste
hot sauce (optional)

SPARE RIBS

Cooking time: 40 minutes.

Cut ribs into pieces with backbone still attached leaving ribs about 4 inches long. Lay on grill or above coals on wire netting. Let the ribs cook for 3 minutes on each side before adding the salt and pepper. If you wish sprinkle the ribs with a little hot sauce then grill until well cooked, about 40 minutes. Do not cook fast, turn every couple of minutes. These are a bush delicacy. Eat with fingers.

You can cook spare ribs in lots of different ways, the above photograph shows them being roasted. This is one of the favourite dishes on all cattle stations the night that they kill their beast for the week's meat.

Jack Absalom.

CASSEROLE OF ANY MEAT OR GAME IN THE BUSH

500 g/1 lb meat
2 slices bacon
1 onion
2 tomatoes
2 dessertspoons peas
½ pint stock or water
1 stick celery
1 carrot
1 level tbl flour
salt and pepper to taste

Cooking time: 2 hours.

Cut meat into slices or pieces and dip into the seasoned flour. Peel and slice the vegetables. Place bacon in dish then half the vegetables, add meat and rest of vegetables. Cook over slow fire for 2 hours.

GYMKHANA HAMBURGERS

1 kg/2 lbs minced meat
2 eggs
1 onion, chopped finely
1 capsicum, chopped finely
1 chilli, chopped finely

Cooking time: ½ hour.

Mix the eggs with the minced meat to bind them. Add the onion, capsicum and chilli. Mould meat into balls, so you can press them into patties. When you place them on the grill plate have about ½ inch thick by 3 inches in diameter. Keep turning until cooked, about 30 minutes. Nice for a barbecue.

DROVERS' DINNER — CORNED BRISKET NORTHERN TERRITORY STYLE

Take best cut off brisket, that is the front piece, about 4 ribs still connected to brisket
salt
water
potatoes
onions

Cooking time: 3½ hours

Take meat and rub well with salt and let stand on some gum leaves over night in a cool place. At daylight bag up away from the flies. Next evening put out to cool. On the

52

third night, or a week after, dip in water and wash off excess salt. Place in a camp oven and boil until cooked, about 3 hours. When meat is cooked wash required amount of potatoes and onions. Then drop them in the meat water and cook. When they are ready carve meat up and serve with the potatoes and onions.

4 thin slices steak, fillet or kangaroo
2 nuts butter
1 dessertspoon parsley
1 tbl hot sauce

BRIDGET'S STEAK DIANNE

Cooking time: 40 minutes

Beat steak with rolling pin or tenderizer until ¼ inch thick. Heat camp oven and drop in a nut of butter. When foaming drop in steak and turn to cook quickly on both sides. Keeping steak flat, put on hot dish, add salt and pepper to taste. Reheat oven. Put in second nut of butter, while foaming add parsley and hot sauce. Pour this sauce over steak and serve at once. Garnish with parsley, and peas if desired.

1 lump of meat 1-1½ kgs/2-3 lbs,
either kangaroo, beef or
mutton

SEASONED POCKET STEAK

Seasoning
¼ loaf bread
1 onion, finely chopped
1 slice bacon, finely chopped
1 tomato, finely chopped
1 egg
salt and pepper to taste

Cooking time: 3 hours.

Take a knife and poke into meat forming a pocket. Now make seasoning, cut crust from bread and crumb. Mix this together with the onion, bacon and tomato. When all mixed add the egg and salt and pepper. Mix well. Stuff this into the pocket of meat. Close up with skewer or sew up. Place in camp oven and bake for 3 hours. Remember if the meat you are using is kangaroo you must baste it every now and then because it has no fat.

NORTH WELL COWBOY STEAK

4 strips bacon
1 kg/2 lbs steak
salt and pepper to taste
2 cups beans

Cooking time: 40 minutes.

Fry bacon until crisp. Place steak on skillet and cook to your choice. When done heat up beans. Arrange steak in middle of plate with bacon on the side and the beans on the other side. Add the salt and pepper.

½ pkt long spaghetti

Sauce
1 kg/2 lbs mince meat
2 onions, chopped finely
2-3 tbls oil or margarine
250 gram tin tomato paste
½ bottle tomato sauce
salt and pepper to taste

Cooking time: 50 minutes.

Heat oil in camp oven. When hot put in the meat and onion. Let this cook for about 20 minutes before adding the tin of tomato paste. When you have added this put in the tomato sauce and salt and pepper. Boil the spaghetti until cooked then take off heat and let it swell in the water. When meat is completely cooked strain the spaghetti and serve.

I have included this recipe in the book especially for all my Italian friends. And I thought it proper that I choose the proper wine.
Jack Absalom.

PIGS CHEEKS CRUMBED

1 pig's head
1 cup flour
2 beaten eggs
1 cup breadcrumbs
dripping or oil

Cooking time: 15 minutes.

Slice the pigs head thinly from the jowls, that is the cheek. When most of the meat is off, dip in flour and then beaten eggs and then breadcrumbs. When all ready have boiling dripping or oil in camp oven. Drop in and cook until brown.

ROAST PORK LEG

1 leg pork
dripping
½ cup water
vegetables (your choice)
1 large tbl flour
2 cups water
1 tbl soya sauce
salt and pepper to taste

Cooking time: 2½-3 hours.

Place the leg of pork with the rind on in a camp oven with some dripping and the water. Keep the camp oven at a steady heat. If the dripping gets too hot add a little more water, so that it has a steaming effect. When cooked add what vegetables you wish. Cook slowly, when ready take out meat and vegetables or leave them in the oven just keeping them warm. If you have too much fat in the oven take some out to make a gravy. Dust in the flour. Keep stirring all the time, if too thick add a little more water. Then lastly add soya sauce, salt and pepper.

ROAST GOAT BRUSHMEN'S STYLE

1 leg or forequarter of goat
cloves of garlic
½ cup plain flour
dripping
1 cup water

Cooking time: 2½-3 hours.

Choose size of leg according to size of camp oven or quantity required. Take cloves of garlic, peel and cut into small

56

pieces. Cut knife well into leg of forequarter and place 5 pieces of garlic into the leg, and a whole piece of garlic for the forequarter if preferred. Dust goat with flour and place in oven with the dripping and a little water. Cook until tender, about 2½-3 hours. Take out and then you can cook the vegetables you wish in hot dripping in camp oven.

There is no meat tastier than roast goat. I always prefer it to mutton, because it is always so much tastier.

Jack Absalom.

Curries

CORNER BEEF CURRY (Drover Style)

dripping
1 kg/2 lbs cooked beef
3 onions
3 potatoes
1 tbls curry powder
½ bottle chutney
½ cup tomato sauce

Cooking time: 45 minutes.

Get dripping hot in camp oven. Dice onions and potatoes and place in camp oven and cook, keep stirring. Don't have too much fat — just enough to keep the vegetables moist. Fry until cooked, testing as you go along. While they are cooking dice the cold meat. When vegetables are ready add the meat and keep stirring until the meat is hot. Add curry powder, and mix well with chutney and tomato sauce. Keep hot until ready to serve. This is a good breakfast served with toast.

DROVERS' CAMP OVEN CURRY

cold meat
2 large potatoes, chopped
2 large onions, chopped
dripping or oil
1 tbls curry powder
1 cup tomato sauce
1 tbls plain flour
water
salt and pepper to taste

Cooking time: 20 minutes.

Cut up any cold meat that you may have, roast, boiled or corned, roughly 1½ cups to each person. Now place the onions and potatoes in the camp oven with a little oil or dripping and fry them. Keep turning until they are cooked. When ready add the meat and keep turning with a fork. When meat is very hot put in curry powder and stir while still very hot and cooking. After 5 minutes drain off fat and add the tomato sauce and the flour, keep stirring. When very hot again put in sufficient water to make enough liquid like a stew. Add salt and pepper. Serve with toast or rice.

1 kg/2 lbs any meat
2½ cups rice
1 small tin pineapple
1 stick celery
2 carrots
2 onions
salt and pepper
1 dessertspoon paprika
2 tbls curry powder
1 tin tomato juice (or small tin puree)
½ cup oil or margarine

CURRY AND RICE

Cooking time: 1½ hours.

Cut off meat, boil till partly cooked then take off gravy. Dice the pineapple, celery, carrot and onions. Fry in oil or margarine until half cooked. Now add paprika and curry powder. Stir for 5 minutes then add tomato juice (or puree) and stir for 2 minutes. Now add gravy from the meat, make enough to cover meat. Allow to put the meat in the same pot as the gravy and with all the vegetables and salt and pepper. Simmer for 1 hour until well cooked. Boil rice and serve with curry.

2 rabbits
1 tbls dripping
2 tbls flour
2 apples, diced
2 tomatoes, diced
1 tbls curry powder
¼ cup tomato sauce
1¼ pints of water
1 tbls rice
1 tbls parsley
salt and pepper to taste

PORT AUGUSTA CURRIED RABBIT

Cooking time: 2½ hours

Joint the rabbits. Heat the dripping in the camp oven and baste rabbits for about 10-15 minutes, then remove. Mix the onions, apples and tomatoes with the flour, curry, tomato sauce and salt and pepper. Place all ingredients into dripping and add water. Stir until it is bubbling then place lid on and cook slowly for 2 hours. When half done add the rice and parsley. Now cook for another hour until tender.

Poultry & Game

COOBER PEDY BRAISED RABBIT

2 medium rabbits
60 g/2 oz dripping
2 large onions
2 tbls plain flour
1 large carrot
2 tomatoes
1 cup peas
salt and pepper to taste

Cooking time: approx. 2-3 hours.

Cut up the rabbit and cook in the dripping until just brown, then take out and place in a dish. Cut the onion into rings and fry in the dripping. If too much dripping pour some out. When onions are 3 parts done then add the flour to make a gravy. When hot, pour water until it makes a thick gravy, add salt and pepper then take off fire and coals and let stand. Clean and dice the carrot along with the tomatoes. Place these over the rabbit with the peas, then pour over the onion gravy. Place on lid of camp oven and cook until the meat is tender on a slow heat. Serve with mashed potatoes.

THE MAIN DIET AT COOBER PEDY IN THE 1920s

1 rabbit
1 tbls dripping
2 onions
water
2 tbls cornflour
salt and pepper

Cooking time: 1½ hours.

Cut up rabbit. Place in camp oven with dripping and braise until brown. Cut up the onions and add when rabbit is brown. As soon as onion is partly done, drain off dripping and cover with water, just enough to simmer. When tender thicken with cornflour and add salt and pepper to taste. Serve with boiled pie melon and annual salt bush. (Just cook the leaves.) The pie melon grew wild. They still service the 20 mile waterhole from Coober Pedy. And the annual salt bush comes with the rain.

60

2 medium-sized rabbits

Gravy
½ cup water
1 dessertspoon cornflour
1 tbls hot sauce
1 tbls tomato sauce
salt and pepper to taste

Short Crust Pastry
4 cups flour
1 cup fat or suet
water

Cooking time: 2½ hours.

Cut up rabbits and place in camp oven. Mix all gravy ingredients together and pour over the rabbit. Put on lid and cook gently for 1 hour. Make the pastry. Place the flour in a bowl and rub the fat or suet into the flour then mix in a little water until you have a nice dough. Roll out to the required size on a floured board. Place pastry over meat in a casserole dish that fits in the camp oven. Cook this for 1½ hours gently.

1 rabbit
3 slices bacon
2 tbls seasoned flour
1 tbls dripping
1 cup water

Stuffing
1 cup breadcrumbs
1 tbls butter or margarine
1 tbls dripping
½ teas thyme
1 teas parsley
1 slice bacon
grated rind of ½ a lemon
salt and pepper to taste

Cooking time: 1½ hours.

Soak rabbit in salt water for ½ hour, drain, then dry. Make stuffing. Rub together butter and breadcrumbs then add all other ingredients, mix well. Fill rabbit with stuffing then

61

fold rabbit in half, bring back legs to front and tie together. Dust rabbit with seasoned flour, lay slice of bacon on top, and put dripping into camp oven. Place rabbit in and cook steadily for 1 hour until the rabbit is well browned on both sides. Serve with gravy and garnish with bacon.

This was probably the most cooked recipe for lots of people through the great depression. Still a favourite with a lot of people.

Roast Stuffed Rabbit.   *Jack Absalom.*

750 g/1½ lbs cooked rabbit
4 tomatoes
3 onions
6 knobs butter or margarine

TIBOOBURRA BUSH CHICKEN

Cooking time: 1½ hours

Prepare seasoning. Dice the tomato and mix with the breadcrumbs and mixed herbs and a sprinkle of salt and pepper. If too dry dampen with a little milk or water. Cut the cold rabbit into pieces and place in the bottom of the camp oven or a dish that will fit in the camp oven. Now slice the onions and tomatoes and spread over the meat. Scatter about ¼ to ½ of the seasoning over the top of the prepared. Now repeat the layers until all ingredients have been used. Top with the knobs of butter and bake for 1½ hours in a moderate camp oven.

OUTBACK FINGER LICKEN RABBIT

1 or 2 rabbits
1 cup plain flour
3 beaten eggs
1½ cups breadcrumbs

Cooking time: 30 minutes.

Cut rabbit into smallish pieces. Roll into the flour, then in the beaten egg then in the breadcrumbs. Have plenty of hot oil or fat in the hot camp oven.When all the rabbit pieces have been crumbed drop them in the hot oil and cook until a rich golden brown. Serve with desired vegetables. Finger Licken Good Tucker.

Reg has been cooking finger licken rabbit for as long as he can remember. Always a great favourite in the bush.

Jack Absalom.

1 duck
3 tbls dripping

Seasoning
½ cup breadcrumbs
1 onion, chopped
1 tomato, chopped
1 egg
mixed herbs
salt and pepper to taste

Cooking time: 1½ hours.

Mix all ingredients for seasoning together and stuff into the duck. Skewer the duck or sew up. Place the duck in a camp oven with the dripping and cook at a moderate heat. If you wish, baste the duck with some honey and soya sauce. It makes the duck beautifully brown. Cook for roughly 1½ hours.

Many drovers I have known over the years always had an old shotgun that they used to get wild ducks for a change of diet. This is a great recipe, and basting them with honey and soya sauce gives them the most wonderful flavour.

Jack Absalom.

ROAST DUCK DROVERS' STYLE

TOAD IN THE HOLE RABBIT

2 rabbits
salt and pepper
60 g/2 ozs dripping

Batter
250 g/½ lb flour
1 egg
pinch salt
milk

Cooking time: approx. 2 hours.

Joint up rabbit and boil in a pot with salt and pepper. When tender take out and drain. Now make the batter by mixing the flour, egg and salt and pepper together slowly adding a little milk at a time until you have a smooth batter. Place dripping in camp oven, when hot drop in rabbit. When rabbit is hot add salt and pepper and pour over batter and bake until cooked, about 40 minutes. Serve with mashed potatoes and peas.

Cooking in Foil

1 chicken cut into quarters
2 tbls oil
salt and pepper to taste
1 onion finely chopped
1 teas garlic powder
¼ cup finely chopped green chilli
2 teas cilantio dried
2 medium chopped tomatoes

Cooking time: 1 hour.

Cut 4, 10 inch squares of heavy foil. Divide the oil amongst the sheets, place a quarter of chicken on each sheet. Salt and pepper to each. Combine all remaining ingredients in a small bowl and mix. Divide over each packet or piece of chicken. Fold and seal. Cook in hot camp oven or in coals for 1 hour.

1 rabbit

Seasoning
½ cup breadcrumbs
1 onion, chopped
2 strips bacon, chopped
1 tomato, chopped
1 egg
salt and pepper to taste

Garnish
2 strips bacon

Cooking time: 2 hours.

Mix all ingredients of seasoning together and stuff into the rabbit. Bring the rabbit's back legs through the front and tie. Lie the rabbit on a large piece of foil. Place the 2 strips of bacon on top for the garnish and seal the foil. Place this into a hot camp oven and cook for 1½-2 hours until cooked. Serve with salad or chips.

**MEAT &
MUSHROOM
PAPOLOTE**

1 kg/2 lbs meat chunks boneless, cut into 1 inch cubes
1 teas monosodium glutomate (optional)
2 cloves garlic, minced
1 cup chopped or dried parsley
2 tbls grated lemon peel
340 g/12 oz mushrooms cleaned and quartered

Cooking time: 1½ hours.

Toss the meat with all the other ingredients. Now spoon mixture onto 6 different pieces of foil, place a little bayleaf in each if required. Close packets. Set them in hot camp oven or on hot coals or in the griller. Keep turning them for about 1½ hours until meat is tender.

Lots of dishes can be cooked in the coals in foil. I find that children get a lot of fun out of cooking their own meal this way. Try it next time.

Jack Absalom.

1½ kgs/3 lbs of fish
1 tbls butter or margarine
2 tbls lemon juice
1 teas tomato to each fish
1 lemon
salt and pepper to taste

SAVOURY OUTBACK FISH IN FOIL

Cooking time: 20 minutes.

Clean and scale fish. Place each fish on a separate piece of foil. Brush each with the melted butter and sprinkle with salt, pepper and lemon juice. Fold and secure foil. Place in hot oven or on hot coals for 20 minutes. Serve from foil.

1 potato per person
½ teas fat per person

ROAST POTATOES IN FOIL

Cooking time: 20-30 minutes.

Wash and rub potatoes with fat. Wrap in foil whole. When soft take out of camp oven or off coals and slice. Add anything else to them that you desire.

6 tomatoes
1½ teas basil
2 tbls butter
1 clove garlic
1½ teas salt
¾ teas pepper

WHOLE TOMATOES IN FOIL

Cooking time: 20 minutes.

Cut off stem ends from tomatoes and squeeze out excess juice and seeds. Place tomatoes right side up each on a separate piece of foil. Sprinkle with pepper and salt, add butter and garlic to each, with a little basil. Seal packets securely and place them in the camp oven. Cook for 20 minutes.

1-1½ kg/2-3 lbs any type fish
foil

YELLOW BELLY

Stuffing
1½ cups soft breadcrumbs
1 tbls parsley (dried/fresh)

69

1 teas mixed herbs
1 teas onion juice
60 g/2 oz butter or margarine
salt and pepper to taste

Cooking time: 1 hour.

Clean and scale fish. Slit open down to the tail. Prepare stuffing. Melt the butter and chop the parsley, mix together with all the other ingredients. Stuff this into each fish and wrap them in foil. Place in hot coals or put in hot camp oven. Bake until tender. When ready open foil and baste with juice, leave open until fish is nice and brown in colour. About 15 minutes.

PINEAPPLE, RICE & HAM PACKET

3 cups cooked rice
1½ tins crushed pineapple
2 spoons brown or white sugar
¼ cup butter or margarine
¼ cup diced green peppers
1 tbls soya sauce
1 teas prepared mustard
250 g/½ lb sliced cooked ham

Cooking time: 15 minutes.

Combine all ingredients together except for the ham. Place the ham on pieces of foil and spread ingredients over each slice. Cook in camp oven or on coals of fire for about 15 minutes.

ZUCCHINI PACKET

6 small zucchini cut cross ways into ¼" slices
1 medium onion, sliced
½ teas salt
¼ teas pepper
1 tbls brown sugar
1 beef cube, crushed
¼ teas crushed fennel seed
3 tbls butter or margarine

Cooking time: 20 minutes.

Place zucchini on centre of foil square. Sprinkle with salt and pepper, beef cube and fennel seed. Dot with butter, wrap and seal. Cook for about 20 minutes.

70

6 large cooking apples
¼ cup raisins
1 tbls grated orange peel
¼ cup honey
¼ cup chopped walnuts
¼ cup orange juice

**BAKED APPLES
IN FOIL**

Cooking time: approx. 30 minutes.

Core and slice off top of apples. About three-quarter fill centre of apples with raisins and nuts. Place apples on piece of foil. Mix orange peel and honey and pour over apples. Now pour orange juice over apples. Wrap in foil, place in camp oven or on hot coals. Cook until apples are tender, approximately 30 minutes. Serve hot or cold with cream.

Vegetables as Side Dishes

CABBAGE — MULYUNGARIE STYLE

cabbage
1 tbls butter
salt and pepper to taste

Cooking time: 1 minute.

Half fill small camp oven with water, bring to the boil. Cut up amount of cabbage required and toss it into the water which will then go off the boil. Watch until it comes to the boil again and then boil for 1 minute. Remove camp oven from the heat and pour the water off. Add the salt and pepper and the butter and stir this until all is mixed through. Place lid on camp oven and let it stand for 5 minutes and then serve.

BALCANOONA POTATO BALLS

2 cups mashed potato
1-2 eggs
¼ cup chopped ham or bacon
1 tbls chopped parsley
salt and pepper to taste
1 cup breadcrumbs

Cooking time: approx. 10 minutes.

Combine all ingredients together and drop spoonfuls into deep hot dripping or oil. After approximately 1 minute remove from heat and shape into balls. Dip these into some beaten egg then roll in breadcrumbs and fry until golden brown.

KETTLE PATIO POTATOES

6 tbls cream
6 pieces heavy duty foil
6 scrubbed potatoes
6 nobs of butter
salt and pepper to taste

Cooking time: 45-60 minutes.

Cut each potato length ways into 4 or 5 slices. Place each sliced potato onto a piece of foil. Pour the cream over each

Potato Balls with Cabbage.

and dot with a nob of butter. Add the salt and pepper and securely wrap each one, folding in the ends. Set in camp oven or on grill and cook for 45-60 minutes at a moderate heat.

VEGETABLE STUFFING
¼ cup margarine
½ cup diced celery
¼ cup diced carrot
¼ cup diced green or red pepper
4 onions, thinly sliced
½ teas salt
¼ teas marjoram leaves, crushed
3 tbls snipped parsley or dried parsley

Cooking time: 10-15 minutes.

Heat margarine in camp oven. Add celery, carrot, peppers and onion, sprinkle with salt. Cook over slow heat for 10-15 minutes. Remove from heat, mix in parsley and dry herbs. Makes about 1 cup of stuffing.

Sauces & Gravies

120 g/4 ozs white breadcrumbs
30 g/1 oz butter
1 blade mace
½ pint milk
1 tbls cream
salt and pepper to taste
sprinkle of cayenne pepper
1 onion diced

BREAD SAUCE

Cooking time: 10 minutes.

Bring milk to the boil add onion and mace and allow to stand by the fire for 20 minutes. Strain milk, return to saucepan, add breadcrumbs and beat well with a fork. Let stand for 10 minutes with lid on then mix in all other ingredients and serve at once.

1 slice of bread per person
1 tbls margarine or butter
1 cup milk
salt and pepper to taste

IRISHMAN'S BREAD SAUCE

Cooking time: 10-15 minutes.

Melt margarine or butter in saucepan, add bread cut into small squares with the crust removed. Now add the milk, salt and pepper and let boil until thick.

1 onion
dried milk
cornflour
1 dessertspoon butter or margarine
salt and pepper to taste

BILL HALLIAN'S ONION SAUCE

Cooking time: 10-15 minutes.

Cut up onion and boil. When cooked make up a mixture of the dried milk, cornflour, salt and pepper with a little water. Mix this into a smooth mixture. Stir into the onion until it becomes creamy, when ready add butter and fold in.

WHITE SAUCE
1 tbls butter
2 tbls cornflour
1½ cups milk
salt and pepper to taste

Melt butter and mix in cornflour. Add the milk, salt and pepper. Keep stirring until it is nice and thick.

TED HOWES' WHITE WINE SAUCE
½ cup white wine
1 tbls lemon juice
1 teas butter
salt and pepper to taste

Mix white wine, lemon juice, butter, salt and pepper together. This sauce is perfect for spreading over fish that is going to be baked in foil.

TARTAR SAUCE
1 cup mayonnaise
2 tbls finely chopped pickles or olives
2 tbls chopped parsley
2 teas lemon juice
salt and pepper to taste

Mix all the ingredients together to a smooth sauce. Very nice.

BAR-BE-QUE SAUCE FOR FISH
1 tbls chilli sauce
1 teas dry mustard
1 tbls butter or margarine
1 tbls worcestershire sauce
sprinkle of garlic salt
salt and pepper to taste

Cooking time: 10-15 minutes.

Combine all ingredients together and make to own taste. Simmer on slow heat then spread over fish.

SPIRO'S BAR-BE-QUE SAUCE
3 onions
2 capsicums
2 tbls margarine
1 teas dry mustard
1 bottle steak sauce

1 medium tin tomato sauce
½ tin dark plum jam
250 gram bottle tomato paste
6 tbls hot sauce
2 cups tomato sauce
1 tbls soya sauce
2 tbls chilli sauce
1 teas tobasco sauce
2 teas salt
¼ teas pepper
1 clove garlic, crushed

Cooking time: 30 minutes.

Place margarine in saucepan or camp oven and heat. Chop onions and capsicums up finely and saute in margarine until tender. Then add all other ingredients and simmer for 15 minutes. Add a little more spices if required.

This recipe is the ultimate in Bar-Be-Que Sauce.

Jack Absalom.

MAYONNAISE

1 tin condensed milk
2 tbls margarine
1½ teas mustard
1 egg
¾ cup vinegar
salt and pepper to taste

Melt the margarine then mix with the mustard. Now add all other ingredients and beat for 20 minutes.

QUICK GRAVY

1 cup water
1 dessertspoon cornflour
1½ tbls hot sauce
1 tbls tomato sauce
salt and pepper
1 tbls port (optional)
½ onion (optional)

Cooking time: 3-5 minutes.

Mix all ingredients together and add the diced onion if wished. Heat in camp oven for 3-5 minutes until boiling.

ROUX 1 large tbls fat
1 tbls flour

Cooking time: 10 minutes.

Place camp oven on hot coals. Put fat inside. When it is melted and hot add the flour, if too dry put in a little more fat so it will bubble. Cook well, but don't burn, 10 minutes will be long enough. You can make plenty of this to keep in the fridge or safe for winter time. Use to thicken stews and gravies and even soups.

PUREE 5.5 kgs/12 lbs over ripe tomatoes
salt

Cooking time: 3-4 hours.

Cut tomatoes open and squash out most of the seeds and liquid, not all, just the watery part. Leave flesh behind, do this until you have done the lot. Put in a bowl, you will notice the excess liquid drain away. When all done place on a piece of clean fly wire, if you do not have a machine for extracting seeds and skin. Now rub all through screen. When complete, bottle and cap tightly. Wrap each bottle with a piece of paper and place in a copper or a large pot that will hold them all. Cover with water and boil for 3 to 4 hours, then let cool in the water. Take out and store. Do not use anything but salt, no spices.

PARISIAN ESSENCE OR VERY DARK COLOURING KNOWN AS BLACK JACK 1 cup sugar

Cooking time: 15-20 minutes.

Have a clean powdered milk tin or a 30 oz fruit tin. Put the sugar in and place on some hot coals, not to boil just so that the sugar will burn. When it is nearly dry pour in a little water, do not overdo it and let boil until it is a liquid. If the mixture is sweet you did not let it burn for long enough. This will keep indefinitely, it is only colour, no taste to worry about, just a black colouring.

GRAVY IN THE CAMP OVEN 1 large tbls fat
1 tbls flour
1 dessertspoon paprika

78

½ pint hot water
1 tbls soya sauce
½ teas salt
¼ teas pepper

Cooking time: 10-12 minutes.

Have camp oven on hot coals. Put fat inside. When melted
and hot add flour and paprika stirring all the time for about
6 minutes. When very hot put water in and keep stirring
until thick. When ready add the soya sauce, salt and pepper. If not dark enough add parisian essence. This gives
a rich colouring. Will keep a long time in the fridge.

1 tbl flour or gravox
½ teas salt
¼ teas pepper
stock or boiling water

GRAVY AFTER ROASTING AND FRYING

Cooking time: 5-10 minutes.

Remove roast meat from baking dish or pan. Strain away
all fat except for about 1½ tlbs. Sprinkle flour or gravox
in the pan, with salt and pepper. Stir well until brown then
add enough stock or boiling water to make gravy required
thickness. If not dark enough, add a little parisian essence.

Desserts

SPOTTED DOG
4 cups S.R. flour
½ cup sugar
1 dessertspoon dripping
1 teas nutmeg
500 g/1 lb currants

Cooking time: 3 hours.

Dissolve the dripping in a pint of hot water. Mix the flour, nutmeg, currants and sugar altogether then add the hot water and dripping, add enough more water as to make a sloppy mix, but not runny. When all mixed put into a cloth—like Christmas pudding and boil for 3 hours. Place a saucer in the bottom of the pot to stop the pudding from burning on the bottom. Make sure the water is boiling before you place the pudding in. Serve with custard.

This is a magnificent recipe and to see it sitting in the middle of a table is really something. It looks wonderful served with custard or cream. It is also very nice fried with butter in a camp oven for breakfast. Reg really excells himself making Spotted Dog.

Jack Absalom.

ALBERT NUNN'S STOCK CAMP STAND-BY
12 slices of bread
butter
jam   oil

Batter
2 cups flour
1 egg
milk
pinch of salt

Cooking time: 5 minutes.

To make batter place flour, salt and egg in a bowl. Add a little milk at a time and mix well together, until you have a smooth paste. Now make six jam sandwiches and cut into quarters. Put the oil in the camp oven and get it hot. When ready dip each quarter piece of sandwich into the batter and then drop into hot oil. Cook until brown, about 4-5 minutes. When ready place on paper and sprinkle with sugar. Four quarters to each person.

80

Spotted Dog.

SAM BROOKS' STEWED QUONDONGS

1 cup sugar
1 kg/2 lbs quondongs

Cooking time: approx. 15-20 minutes.

Place quondongs in saucepan or camp oven and cover with water and the sugar. Boil until tender, about 15-20 minutes. Pour into a container and let cool. Serve with plenty of fresh or tinned cream.

Sam Brooks was the man who discovered Andamooka Opal Fields. Many times over the years they struggled to survive, and this recipe was one of their favourites.

Jack Absalom.

NULLARBOR GINGER ROLL

½ cup sugar
½ cup S.R. flour
2 eggs
1 tbls milk
1 tbls water
1 dessertspoon ground ginger

Cooking time: 20 minutes.

Beat eggs well, add sugar and beat well again. Pour in milk and water then sift in flour with ground ginger and mix. Bake in a shallow greased tin or tray. When cooked lay on a damp cloth. Spread some mock cream in the centre and then roll up.

BUSH MOCK CREAM

2 tbls powdered milk
¼ cup sugar
1 large tbls cornflour
170 g/6 ozs soft butter
1 teas vanilla essence

Cooking time: approx. 5-10 minutes.

Place a pint of water on the boil. Mix in a small bowl the powdered milk, sugar and cornflour. Mix up cornflour with a little water to take out the lumps before you mix it with the other ingredients. When water has boiled stir in the mixture until fairly stiff. Take off heat and let cool until cold. When cold skim off top skin then add the butter. Beat well then add vanilla essence.

½ or ¼ melon
1 cup sugar
2 cups rice

**PIE MELON
AND RICE
SWEETS**

Cooking time: approx. 15 minutes.

Dice up melon required. Take out seeds and stew until tender with sugar added. Put into dish and let cool. Boil the rice, when cooked wash off starch and cool. Serve pie melon with rice. Very tasty.

3 tbls custard powder
½ cup sugar
1 cup Sunshine powdered milk
vanilla essence

**CREAMY
CUSTARD**

Cooking time: 10-15 minutes.

Mix custard powder, sugar and Sunshine milk together with a little water until you have a fine texture. Place saucepan on coals with water in and bring to the boil. When boiling pour in the prepared mixture slowly stirring all the time until you have a creamy custard. Now add the vanilla essence. Serve hot or cold.

2½ cups flour
3 tbls dripping or butter
1½ teas baking powder
1 teas sugar
pinch of salt

**JIM SHAW'S
BOILED JAM
ROLL**

Cooking time: 1½-2 hours.

Mix all ingredients to a stiff dough. Roll out neatly square onto a clean tea-towel. Spread dough thinly with a little of your favourite jam. Roll up in a tea towel and fasten with a safety pin or pins. Drop into boiling water and boil for 1½-2 hours. Serve with cream.

Very good dessert for a change from the usual ones. I like it with cream or custard.

Jack Absalom.

HILLMAN'S APRICOT SLICE

3 cups stewed apricots or 1 large tin apricots

Pastry
170 g/6 ozs butter
2 eggs
2 cups S.R. flour
120 g/4 ozs castor sugar

Cooking time: approx. 30 minutes.

To make the pastry mix the butter and sugar together, then add the eggs and the flour. Knead the mixture. The dough will be fairly hard to handle. Halve the dough and roll out on a floured board. Lay one half of pastry on the bottom of the pie dish, cover in apricots with the juice strained off and a little sugar. Cover with remaining pastry and trim around the edges. Prick the top of the pie and paint with a beaten egg. Bake until it is nice and brown, about 30 minutes.

This is a wonderful recipe to make. Mrs Hillman lived at Andamooka Opal Fields, she cooked these to perfection.
Jack Absalom.

84

Jam

Pastry
250 g/½ lb flour
pinch of salt
120 g/4 oz margarine or butter
½ cup water
1 teas sugar

Glaze
1 beaten egg

Cooking time: approx. 1 hour.

Sift flour into a bowl and add the salt and sugar. Rub in margarine with tips of fingers and pour in the water, cold as you can get it. Make this into a soft dough. Roll out on floured board and dampen the edges. Spread with jam of your choice and roll up. Glaze with a beaten egg and bake in a moderate oven for about 1 hour.

This is a wonderful way to present a jam roll at a children's party.
Looks really something on the table.

Jack Absalom.

BAKED DAMPER CUSTARD

6 slices damper
butter
jam
¼ cup sugar
1 pint milk
nutmeg

Cooking time: approx. 20-30 minutes.

Cut off crust from damper. Spread with butter and jam, place in the bottom of a pie dish. Mix together the sugar and milk and cover the prepared in pie dish. Sprinkle a little nutmeg on top and cook till set and brown.

Pastries

250 g/½ lb flour
pinch of salt
120 g/4 ozs clear fat or butter
½ cup water
1 teas sugar (only needed for sweet dishes)

PASTRY (Short Crust)

Sift flour, add salt and sugar if for sweet dish. Rub in fat or butter with tips of fingers. Pour the water in the centre slowly making a stiff dough that will leave the sides of the dish clearly. Tip out onto floured board and knead slowly with tips of fingers and thumbs. Then turn rough side down and roll out to required size.

3 cups flour
1½ cups margarine (cold)
flour for dusting
little chilled water

FLAKY PASTRY

Mix the flour with a little water at a time until you have a nice thin dough. Roll it out. Take ½ cup of cold margarine and spread it over the pastry, then sprinkle with a little flour and fold three times. Roll the dough out again and repeat spreading the margarine with another ½ cup. Fold three times again, roll out and use the remaining ½ cup margarine. Dust with flour and fold three times. Now roll the dough out and it is ready for your requirements.

3 apples
cinnamon and sugar to taste
1 egg

APPLE TURNOVER

Cooking time: 20-30 minutes.

Make the *Short Crust Pastry*. Roll out about 12 inches square. Dampen edges with a little water. Place apples which have been peeled and grated in the middle of the pastry. Sprinkle with sugar and cinnamon and roll up. Place in a dish or tray and paint with a beaten egg. Bake in hot oven for 20-30 minutes. Serve with hot custard. Very delicious.

KIDMAN'S JAM TART

¾ cup jam

Cooking time: 15 minutes.

Make a Short Crust Pastry as shown in the recipe above. Roll out to plate size. Place pastry in the bottom of the pie dish and cover with the jam. Bake in hot oven for 15 minutes.

A favourite on Kidman's Station. Especially when they had sold a big mob of cattle.

Jack Absalom.

500 g/1 lb peaches
½ cup sugar
1 tbls gelatine

**WILD PEACH
FLAN**

Cooking time: 30 minutes.

Stew the peaches. Place them in a saucepan with the sugar.
Cover with water and boil till soft—about 15 minutes. When
ready strain off liquid and keep in saucepan. Add gelatine
to the liquid and keep warm until well dissolved. Now make
the *Short Crust Pastry* which is rolled out to the required
size and place in the bottom of a pie dish. Prick or pinch
the bottom of the pastry to stop it from rising. Bake in a
hot oven until nice and brown, about 15 minutes. Take out
of the oven and let cool. When cool arrange the peaches
on the pastry and cover with the juice. Let stand and cool.
When set serve with bush cream.

CUSTARD TART (Bush Way)

1 egg
milk
custard powder
sugar

Cooking time: 15 minutes.

Make the *Short Crust Pastry*. Roll out and place in the bottom of a pie dish. Prick the bottom of the dough or pastry to stop it from rising. Paint with beaten egg and bake in a hot oven for about 15 minutes until brown. Take out and let cool. Make a mixture of custard using milk, custard powder and sugar. When ready pour into prepared pastry case and let cool. Serve with fruit or by itself.

ZANTHUS WILD PEACH ROLL

500 g/1 lb peaches
½ cup sugar
1 egg

Cooking time: 30 minutes.

Stew peaches. Place in saucepan and cover with water and the sugar. Boil until they are soft. Drain off the juice and let stand and cool. Make a *Short Crust Pastry*. Roll out fairly square and dampen the edges with a little milk or water. Spread the peaches over the pastry about 1½ inches from the edges. Roll up loosely. Place on a tray. Paint with beaten egg and bake in a hot oven until brown. Serve with custard.

NARETHA QUONDONG PIE

1 kg/2 lbs quondongs
1 cup sugar
1 egg

Cooking time: 30 minutes.

Remove stones from quondongs. Place in a saucepan and cover with water and the sugar. Stew until soft about 15 minutes. When cooked place in a pie dish. Make the *Short Crust Pastry*. Cover the quondongs with the pastry and paint with beaten egg. Bake in a hot oven for about 15 minutes until pastry is brown. Serve with cream when cold and custard when hot.

90

½ cup jam
1½ cups dates
1 egg

**KINGOONYA
DATE SLICE**

Cooking time: 20-30 minutes.

Make the *Short Crust Pastry*. Cut dough in halves and roll out both pieces. Place one piece in a flat dish and spread with the jam and cut up dates. Place second piece of pastry on the top to cover. Press around the edges. Prick the top with a fork and paint with beaten egg. Bake in a hot oven for about 20-30 minutes. When cooked dust with sugar or icing sugar.

1 dessertspoon cinnamon
1 dessertspoon sugar
1½-2 cups currants

**RAWLINA
CURRANT
TURNOVER**

Cooking time: 20-30 minutes.

Make the *Short Crust Pastry*. Roll out square. Put currants in a strainer and pour boiling water over them and drain. Sprinkle cinnamon and sugar on currants. Place the currants on the dough and turn dough over like a sandwich. Bake in camp oven for about 20-30 minutes, until nice and brown. Take out and paint with boiling water and sugar.

Cakes & Biscuits

CAMPERS'
FRUIT CAKE

1 kg/2 lbs mixed fruit
1 large cup water (cold)
pinch of salt
nuts if desired
1 large cup brown sugar
2 teas spices
3 eggs
1 pkt pastry mix

Cooking time: 2½ hours.

Place all ingredients except for eggs and pastry mix into a saucepan and boil for 3 minutes. When this is cool add eggs that have been well beaten. Now add pastry mix and mix together well. Place all mixture into a well greased and lined cake tin and bake in a moderate oven for 2½ hours approximately.

8 eggs
1½ cups sugar
1½ cups S.R. flour
½ cup cornflour
1 heaped teas cream of tartar
1 level teas carb soda
orange flavouring or grated orange peel from 2 oranges

Cooking time: 20-30 minutes.

Mix together eggs, sugar, cream of tartar and carb soda, then sift in the flour and cornflour and mix all together, along with the orange flavouring, gently with a knife. When ready pour mixture into a greased cake tin or in the camp oven. Cook in moderate camp oven for 20-30 minutes.

ORANGE SPONGE CAKE BUSH STYLE

COOPERS CREEK BROWNIE CAKES

2 cups water
2 cups mixed fruit
2 cups sugar
2 tbls butter
4 cups plain flour
1 teas bicarb soda
spices
pinch of cinnamon
pinch of salt

Cooking time: approx. 1 hour.

Mix water, mixed fruit, sugar and butter together then boil for 5 minutes and let cool. Now add flour, bicarb soda, spices, cinnamon and salt. Mix well and put in small bread tin or cake tin. Cook in camp oven.

NARYILCO HOT CAKES

250 g/½ lb flour
2 dessertspoons baking powder
2 eggs or 1 large tbls custard powder
1 cup milk

Cooking time: 10-15 minutes.

Mix all ingredients into a thick batter. Drop into hot camp oven with a little fat or oil. Bake until a light golden brown. These are very tasty and are used as sweets. They also make a nice hot cake with the breakfast dishes.

STURT'S STONEY DESERT GIBBER CAKES

90 g/3 ozs butter
90 g/3 ozs sugar
1 egg
¼ cup milk
225 g/8 ozs flour
2 level teas baking powder
1 handful of currants, sultanas or raisins

Cooking time: 10-15 minutes.

Beat butter and sugar until creamy and then add all other ingredients, make into a dough. Break off pieces with a fork and drop into a greased camp oven and bake for about 10-15 minutes.

94

1 cup coconut
1 cup S.R. flour
1½ cups cornflakes
½ cup sultanas
¼ cup wheatgerm (optional)
¼ cup chopped dates (optional)
1 cup treacle or golden syrup
½ cup margarine

Cooking time: 10-15 minutes.

Mix all dry ingredients together. If adding the dates chop them finely. Melt the margarine and golden syrup in a saucepan. When this starts to bubble take off the heat and add to dry ingredients a bit at a time mixing well. After you have mixed in all the margarine and golden syrup you should have a nice moist mixture. Drop spoonfuls of this into a heated greased camp oven that is at a moderate temperature. Cook until light brown, about 10-15 minutes. Take out and allow to set, about 15 minutes.

April is my youngest daughter, she excels herself making these in the camp oven. They even taste good.

Jack Absalom.

Dumplings, Scones & Bread

DUMPLINGS (for sweets and stews)

3 cups flour
1 dessertspoon baking powder
1 teas fat
pinch salt

Cooking time: 20 minutes.

Rub fat in the flour with fingers, then add luke-warm water to make a soft dough that you can roll into balls, about the size of a small apple. Leave them on the floured board until they have all been rolled. Now you can pop them into your boiling water, or on the top of your stew. When they are in the pot just let them simmer, not boiling hard. Keep the lid on just so you can see them bubbling on the edge of the pot for 20 minutes. The plain boiled dumplings are nice with honey or golden syrup over them. The others are delicious in stews.

PUFF-A-LOONS

fat or oil
3 cups flour
1 dessertspoon baking powder
½ cup water

Cooking time: 5-10 minutes.

Place the required camp oven on the coals. Not a big shovel full of coals, just enough to get hot. Make a dough of flour, baking powder and water. Mix into a dough and roll out. Cut into squares, drop into 1 inch of fat or oil in camp oven. When they are puffed up and light brown in colour lift out and drop next lot in. These can be eaten with meat, jam, honey or treacle. Or even by themselves as bread.

SODA BREAD

6 cups plain flour
1 teas salt
2 teas bicarb soda
45 g/1½ ozs butter or margarine
1 teas cream of tartar
1 dessertspoon baking powder

Dumplings and Golden Syrup.

Cooking time: 20-30 minutes.

Sift and mix all dry ingredients, rub in butter with finger tips then pour in a little milk to make a nice spongy dough. Mould this into rolls or loaves as you require them. Let stand for ½ hour then place in a moderate oven for about 20-30 minutes, until nice and brown.

You can use this mixture for soda scones. To make bread use the same as soda bread, adding ½ handful currants to dry mixture.

SHORT BREAD

170 g/6 ozs butter
120 g/4 ozs castor sugar
2 eggs
2 cups S.R. flour
sufficient flour to roll

Cooking time: approx. 20 minutes.

Mix butter and sugar. Add eggs and then the flour sifted. Knead mixture. It will be fairly hard to handle. Roll out and add what you want. Bake in moderate oven for about 20 minutes.

ON THE ROAD BUNS

1.5 kg/3 lbs flour
1½ pints tepid water
30 g/1 oz compressed yeast
4 tbls home made yeast
2 tbls brewer's yeast
4 teas sugar
2 teas salt
30 g/1 oz butter
1 teas mixed spices
1 cup mixed fruit or sultanas

Cooking time: 10-15 minutes.

Sift and warm 1.25 kg/2½ lbs flour, make a well in the centre. Beat yeast and sugar with 250g/½ lb flour and let it rise a bit. After 20 minutes pour into centre of dough with water and knead well. After 1 hour flatten a bit, then add the melted butter, mixed fruit and mixed spices. Knead well then put in tins or cut into loaves and cook in camp oven. When ready glaze with boiled water and sugar.

98

60 g/2 ozs butter
½ cup sugar
1 egg
1 cup cold mashed pumpkin
2 cup S.R. flour

PUMPKIN SCONES

Cooking time: 15 minutes.

Cream the butter and sugar, add eggs and pumpkin. Add sifted flour and mix well. Cut into 1½ inch squares and place in greased camp oven and bake for 15 minutes.

2 cups S.R. flour
pinch salt
2 teas butter
1 cup milk

BIRDSVILLE SCONES

Cooking time: 7-10 minutes.

Sift the flour and salt, rub butter into flour. Add sufficient milk to make a soft dough, put on floured board and knead very lightly. Roll dough out, about ¾ inch thick. Cut into shapes. Garnish them with milk and place in hot camp oven for 7-10 minutes.

1.5 kg/3 lbs flour
1½ pints tepid water
30 g/1 oz compressed yeast
4 tbls home made yeast
2 level tbls brewers yeast
4 teas sugar
2 teas salt

BREAD

Cooking time: large 1 hour
small ½ hour.

Sift and warm 1.25 kg/2½ lbs of the flour and make a well in the centre. Beat yeast and sugar with a tbls flour and let rise a bit. After 20 minutes pour into centre of dough with tepid water and knead well. After 1 hour put on floured board and knead into loaves or rolls. Place in camp oven and let rise a bit until they are double their size. Bake in hot camp oven for about 40-50 minutes depending on the size of the rolls, large 1 hour, small ½ hour. The bread

Bread should have a hollow sound when you tap the bottom, let cool upside down.
And don't work dough in the wind when making bread.

STRZELECKI DAMPER

6 cups S.R. flour
1 tbls baking powder
pinch salt
warm milk

Cooking time: approx. ½ hour.

Mix flour, baking powder, salt and warm milk into a nice dough. If doubtful keep out a couple cups of flour and make the dough wet, then add the dry flour to make a spongy dough. Place the camp oven on the fire and make it hot before you put the bread mix in. When hot place the camp oven over the coals and place the mixture in. Put lid on camp oven and cover it with hot coals. Bake damper for approximately ½ hour.

I never cook damper unless I have no yeast at all. I honestly believe that everybody I know in the outback prefers bread, but they cook damper because bread takes a little longer and it is just a little more trouble. Most people take the easy way out and make a damper, but all of them, without exception, prefer bread, which most of them can't cook. I will probably get a lot of complaints over this statement but it is true, even though they will not admit it.

Jack Absalom.

Strzelecki Damper

Batters

BASIC BATTER MIXTURE
120 g/4 ozs S.R. flour
pinch of salt
¼ pint of tepid water
1 tbls melted butter
1 egg white

Sift flour into basin, make a well in the middle of the flour. Pour in the butter and gradually add the water. Beat well. Beat egg white until light and fluffy, fold into batter just before using.

SECOND BATTER MIXTURE
2 cups S.R. flour
pinch of salt
1 egg
a little milk

Mix all ingredients together with a little milk until creamy. If using this batter for sweets add a little sugar.

PANCAKE BATTER
1 cup plain flour
¼ teas salt
1 egg
1¼ cups milk

Cooking time: 12 minutes.

Mix the egg, milk and salt together then sift in the flour. Beat mixture well by hand until small bubbles appear on top. Let this stand for at least 30 minutes before using. When you are ready to cook pour the mixture, about 2 tbls at a time into a greased camp oven. The oven must be hot. Cook until each side is golden brown.

BANANA FRITTERS
4 bananas
sugar
oil

Cooking time: 5-10 minutes.

Peel and slice the bananas. Make the *Basic Batter Mixture*

that is shown in the above recipe. Have the camp oven on the fire with plenty of hot oil. Dip banana pieces in the batter and drop them in the hot oil. Fry until they are a nice golden brown colour. When you take them out sprinkle them with sugar and they are ready for serving. You can even substitute the bananas for pineapple or apples.

Banana Fritters.

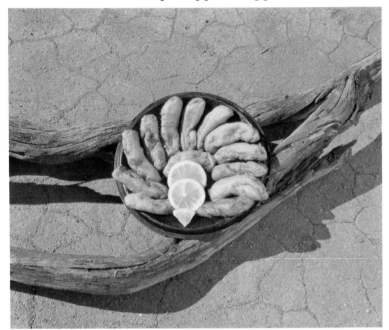

Yeasts

BAKERS YEAST I myself used compressed yeast — that is what the bakers use. You can get it from the bakers or health food shops. Use a half-inch slice to 6 loaves of bread. It is wrapped like a pound of butter.

Reg Absalom.

ACID YEAST 1 medium potato
1½ tbls sugar
½ teas citric or tartaric acid
1 cup warm water
2 teas flour

Cooking time: approx. 15 minutes.

Boil and mash potato, add all ingredients and sufficient water to keep mixture at a cup full. Bottle or put in a jar and cork tightly. Keep in a warm place. 12 hours in an old yeast jar, if not 24 hours at least in a new jar.

OODNADATTA YEAST BUNS YEAST MIXTURE
½ inch thick slice compressed yeast
1 cup flour
luke warm water

Place compressed yeast into a bowl and add flour and crumble together. Add enough luke warm water to make a watery paste. Let stand for 1 hour until it rises.

BUN MIXTURE 1½ sifts flour or 6 cups
½ cup sugar
½ cup currants or sultanas
1 teas nutmeg
2 pints milk
1 dessertspoon butter or margarine
2 eggs
lemon essence

Cooking time: approx. 15 minutes.

104

Mix together the flour, sugar, currants and nutmeg, let stand. Warm the milk so it is hot enough that the butter you have placed in it will melt, mix well. When cool add the beaten eggs and a little lemon essence.

When yeast mixture is ready make a well in the flour, add fruit mixture, and add in yeast and milk mixture. Mix this all together until you have a soft dough that you can knead. If too wet add a little more flour or if too dry add a little water or milk. Stand in a warm place for 1 hour.

When dough has risen empty onto a floured board and knead. Cut off about 700 g/1½ lbs and roll into a long sausage length, 1½ inches round. Now cut the sausage dough into 2 inch pieces and mould them into balls. Place on a greased tray, or in a greased camp oven. Let them rise until they are double their size and then bake them for about 15 minutes. When cooked and golden to light brown take out and glaze with heated sugar. Place a saucepan on heat with ½ cup sugar and boil for 10-15 minutes. Then brush on buns or any other sweet dishes.

HOP YEAST

1 large potato
1 pint of water (rain water if you have it)
1 teas hops
1 tbls flour
1 tbls sugar

Cooking time: 20 minutes.

Boil potato, add hops while still boiling. Boil for 20 minutes. Strain and cool slightly, add flour and sugar. Bottle and cork tightly.

The yeast should work in a few hours if you used a bottle that previously had yeast in it. 24 hours in a new bottle. Raisins or sultanas will hurry up the yeast, use only one or two raisins or sultanas.

COOBER PEDY FINGERS

Make the same mixture as for Yeast Buns leaving out the currants.

Cooking time' 15-20 minutes.

After the dough has risen place on floured board, cut in half and roll out to a ½ inch thickness then even up the pieces. Cut it into long strips about 5 inches in length. Place on greased tray and let rise for ½ hour. Then bake in camp oven for 15-20 minutes. Put on plate or tray and glaze before they get too cold. Wipe over with thin pink or white icing.

TORPEDO BUNS

Prepare yeast as in Yeast Buns recipe.
2 sifts flour or 8 cups plain flour
½ cup sugar
2 teas nutmeg
2 eggs
1 dessertspoon margarine
3 tbls powdered milk

Cooking time: ½ hour.

Mix margarine with hot water to dissolve. When cool add beaten eggs and powdered milk, making about 2 pints. Add all dry ingredients to flour and mix well. Add yeast after it has risen, then milk and egg mixture. If you do not have enough liquid to make a soft dough add a little more milk. Let this rise for about 1 hour on a floured board. When risen roll out into torpedo shapes and place them on greased trays. Now let rise again for about ¾ hour. Place in oven and cook until brown. Put on wire tray and glaze with boiling water and sugar. When cool run a strip of icing down the centre of the torpedos and sprinkle with coconut.

It is marvellous how much difference it makes when presenting yeasts, to ice them with a little coconut sprinkled on top.
                                                                    Jack Absalom.

1 sift flour or 4 cups
¼ cup sugar
1 teas cinnamon
1 teas mixed spices

Cooking time: 15 minutes.

Prepare yeast as in *Yeast Buns* and let rise or ferment for
¾ hour. Make a hole in the flour and add the yeast. Have
ready some luke-warm water, stir in gradually until you
have a nice spongy dough. Knead well and let rise until
double the size. Tip out onto floured board and knead until
not sticky. Cut in half, roll out with hands to make a long
sausage, then curl around to make knot in dough. Place
on tray or in camp oven. Repeat the same procedure with
the other half of the dough. Let rise for ¾ hour then bake
in hot oven. When lightly brown test it by pushing down
on the dough with fingers, if it does not come back again
cook until it rises back. Glaze with boiling water and sugar,
then dust with icing sugar or decorate with icing and dust
with coconut.

Pickles, Chutneys & Brines

BUSHMEN'S BOTTLING AND PRESERVING OUTFIT

Wrap jars and bottles with a piece of newspaper to stop from breaking and banging together. When boiling, stand all bottles and jars upright. I have used this method for years.

Reg Absalom.

GREEN TOMATO PICKLES

3 kgs/6 lbs green tomatoes
1 kg/2 lbs onions
70 g/2½ ozs salt
700 g-1 kg/1½-2 lbs sugar
½ bottle easysauce
1 dessertspoon mustard
1 dessertspoon curry powder
1 dessertspoon cornflour
1 teas tumeric

Cooking time: 1 hour.

Slice the tomatoes and onions into a dish. Add the salt and let this stand for 12 hours. Now empty the contents into a pan and bring to the boil before adding the sugar and easysauce. Boil for one hour until thick enough. Mix mustard, curry powder, cornflour and tumeric into a paste, add this to the mixture before the end of the boiling time. When ready jar up and store away.

CURRY POWDER — YOUR OWN SPECIAL MIXTURE

500 g/1 lb curry powder
1 kg/2 lbs coriander powder
500 g/1 lb skinned garlic
6 bayleaves
350 g/12 ozs chilli powder
60 g/2 ozs cayenne pepper

Place curry powder in a bowl, add the coriander powder and the skinned garlic. Put this through a mincer. Now put in the bayleaves, chilli powder and cayenne pepper. Mix this altogether and leave in the open dish for 2 days, mixing every now and again, so that the wet garlic does not make the rest of the mixture go mouldy. Now place in jars and cap tightly.

4 kgs/9 lbs tomatoes
1·4 kgs/3 lbs onions
85 g/3 ozs salt
500 g/1 lb apples
1.2 kg/2½ lbs sugar
½ bottle easysauce
1½ tbls mustard
1½ tbls curry powder
1½ tbls cornflour
1½ tbls tumeric
15 g/½ oz mace
15 g/½ oz cloves
15 g/½ oz allspice
7 g/¼ oz chillies
15 g/½ oz pepper
30 g/1 oz ginger

PORTANA CHUTNEY

Cooking time: 1½-2 hours.

Slice tomatoes and onions. Add salt and dice apples. Place all this in a dish and let stand for 12 hours. Empty contents into a large pan or stew pot. Bring to the boil before adding the sugar and easysauce. Boil until nice and thick — 1½ hours or maybe longer. Now add together and make into a paste mustard, curry powder and tumeric. Add this paste to the other mixture 10 minutes before taking off the boil. Jar up and store away.

15 g/½ oz mace
15 g/½ oz cloves
15 g/½ oz allspice
7 g/¼ oz chillies
15 g/½ oz pepper
30 g/1 oz ginger

EASYSAUCE

Mix all ingredients together and you have easysauce.

38 litres/10 gallons water
salt
1 potato
1 lb brown sugar or ¾ tin treacle
120 g/4 ozs slick peter or kwik cure

BRINE FOR PICKLING

Place water in large pot. Add potato to the water. Add salt

until the potato floats to the top of the water. Stir while adding the salt. Now add the sugar or treacle along with the kwik cure. Mix well, keep in a cool place. Now add meat such as pork flaps, sheep, goat or kangaroo legs. Leave for about 5 days then it is ready to cook. Corn goat flaps, sheep and pig belly pork. Serve with onion sauce and vegetables of your own choice.

STOCKMAN'S BRINE

15 litres/4 gallons water
1 potato
salt
250 g/½ lb brown or white sugar or ½ tin of treacle
2 dessertspoons salt and pepper or 1 tbls kwik cure

This is used for pickling mutton, beef or pork. Place water in a large pot. Add potato to the water. Now add salt until the potato floats. Keep stirring as you add the salt, when the potato floats then take it out. Add the sugar or treacle with the kwik cure. This mixture will keep for months in a cool place.